To: Ann. R.
Diamond

From: Joan R.
Powers

MODERNes

ISBN: 0-8362-5105-9

Together in Time

Art by Erika and Theresa Carter
Written by J. Sturgis Miller

**Andrews McMeel
Publishing**

Kansas City

We've
shared
great
memories
over the
years...

as we've grown

closer

through the

bond of

friendship.

You have

given me

the freedom

of a

lightened heart...

by being
a trusted friend
in whom
to confide my
deepest feelings.

Through
the years
you have
eased my troubles
and dried
my tears...

...your comfort

was always

with me.

You were there
for my joys
and triumphs,
my successes
and celebrations.

t. Carter

The dearest gift
I have
is the gift
you give
of yourself.

Timeless
and constant,
your friendship
is something
I cherish.

And it is

the simple things

I value

the most...

...our humor,

our honesty,

our openness.

We are

lasting friends.

Our history is
a rich tapestry
woven of
precious moments...

warming

our hearts

as we walk

toward tomorrow...

Together

in

time.

The Carter sisters: Theresa and Erika

The Modernes greeting books feature
the modern impressionistic artwork of
sisters and fellow artists, Theresa and
Erika Carter. The Carter sisters are
second generation Santa Barbarans
from a large and artistic family.
As children they were surrounded by a
wide variety of art, cultivating within
them a strong sense of design and
aesthetics. As adults, their passion for
expression continues and their work is
enjoyed by art collectors nationwide.